HOPI KACHINA DOLLS

MUSEUM *of*
NORTHERN
ARIZONA

FORM & FUNCTION IN HOPI TITHU
by Robert Breunig and Michael Lomatuway'ma

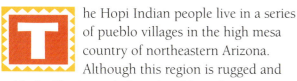

The Hopi Indian people live in a series of pueblo villages in the high mesa country of northeastern Arizona. Although this region is rugged and arid, the Hopi people have lived here for centuries—traditionally subsisting on such staples as corn, beans, and squash. Farming on the land requires great skill and an intimate understanding of the characteristics of the environment, for such forces as frost, hail, flash floods, high winds, and drought often combine to threaten crops.

The traditional religious system of the Hopi reflects their dependence upon and sensitivity to the precarious nature of this agriculture. Over the years, the Hopi have developed a set of annual ceremonies that emphasize the fertility, germination, growth, and maturity of their crops. All of these ceremonies, which are conducted by a number of ceremonial groups or societies, focus on the ever-present need for rain. Most of these groups have an exclusive membership. However, one group includes any willing initiated member of the Hopi tribe, and it is the male members of this group (along with the members of the more exclusive Powamuy Society) that perform the most visible and pervasive of the Hopi ceremonials—those of the kachina cult. (Note: the word kachina is linguistically more correct if spelled *katsina* or, if plural, *katsinam*.)

The kachina ceremonies reflect the traditional Hopi view of their universe. A fundamental theme of their world view is that the universe is divided into two realms: the upper world of the living and the lower world of spirits. Events occur between these two worlds in alternating and regular cycles. For example, the sun moves between the upper world by day and the lower world by night on its daily course.

Likewise, it follows an alternating cycle through the year. As the days grow longer between the winter and summer solstices, the sun's energies bring germination and growth to the upper world. This could be called the traditional "summer" season. As the days wane between the summer solstice and the winter solstice, it becomes "winter" in the upper world but "summer" in the spirit world since their world is a mirror reflection of this one. Similarly, there is a cycle for an individual: one is born, lives, dies, and goes to the spirit realm—to be reborn. While the dead are in the spirit world, they continue to act as members of society.

These ancestor spirits (and also the spirits of the animals, plants, and other objects in the Hopi natural world) are the kachinas. As supernaturals, they act by carrying the prayers of the living to the deities or by interceding with the forces of nature to promote that which sustains life on the earth.

The period between the winter solstice to just past the summer solstice is the kachina season. During the other half of the year, the kachinas return to their own realm in the spirit world upon Nuvatukya'ovi (the San Francisco Peaks to the southwest of the Hopi mesa) and other places associated with water or moisture. These other places include Kawestima (Betatakin Ruin), Kiisiwu (a spring to the northeast), and Weenima (near Zuni) to the southeast.

OPPOSITE: *Mastopkatsina* (E977)
In days past, a pair of these kachinas visited Old Oraibi during *Soyalangw*, the winter solstice ceremony.

ABOVE: The San Francisco Peaks are sacred to the Hopi. Photograph by Tom Brownold

While the Hopi have a year-long set of religious activities, it is only during the kachina season that these rites feature kachinas. The one exception to this rule is the *Masawkatsina*, which can appear in the non-kachina season.

There are many kachinas, and each has its own characteristics such as personality, call or hoot, costume, song style, and set of body movements that can be identified easily. Most are considered benevolent friends; some are funny, but others are ogres and monsters who come to threaten children.

Kachinas change in popularity over the decades. Some have not appeared for years; a few have been dropped completely, while others have been added to the pantheon relatively recently. Because kachinas come and go over the years, it is not possible to establish an exact number.

Kachinas are named in a variety of ways. Some are named after the spirit or animal they represent—such as *Sootukwnangw* (the sky spirit or god) or *Honankatsina* (badger kachina). Some are named after the sounds they emit—such as the *Hoote* kachina, who makes the sound "hoootee" when entering a kiva, the village plaza, or repairing to dance. Others are named for an attribute of their mask, such as *Payuk'ala* or "three-horned kachina," *Kwikwilyaqa*, "striped nose" or *Angwusnasomtaqa* ("one who has crow feathers as a hairdo"). Some are named for the way that they move—such as *Ngayayataqa* or "one who sways back and forth." Still others are named for some specific aspect of their character, for example, *Suyang'ephoya*, the left-handed kachina. Kachinas are even named after the person who first sponsored their appearance at a dance. A number of names, such as *Qööqöqlö* or *Hoo'e*, are untranslatable into English.

Hee'e'wuuti (E960)
Often called "warrior woman" in English, this kachina leads a Bean Dance procession of kachinas in a *qöqöntinumya* ("going round and round") at the Hotevilla Bean Dance.

HOPI CEREMONIAL CYCLE

There is some variation in the manner in which kachinas appear. Some (like the *Soyalkatsina* or *Eototo*) appear within the context of specific ceremonies—such as the *Soyalangw* (winter solstice) or Powamuy (Bean Dance) ceremonies. Others are seen only in association with other types of kachinas or in their specialized roles of guards, runners, or side dancers at the dances. Most kachinas, however, come in large groups that appear as a single line of dancers. These lines usually are composed of just one type of kachina. Less frequently, mixed types of kachinas appear in line formations.

THE CEREMONIAL YEAR

The first ceremonial event of the year in which the kachinas can appear is the winter solstice ceremony or *Soyalangw*. This ceremony marks the return of the sun to its "winter house." Now the days grow longer, and preparations begin for the planting season to come. Therefore, fertility is one of the major themes of the *Soyalangw*. *Paahos*, or prayer sticks with attached feathers that embody messages to the supernaturals, are prepared in prayers for well-being and abundance.

At the end of *Soyalangw*, the kivas (underground religious structures) are opened for a series of night-time kachina dances. At most of these dances, groups representing different kiva membership migrate from kiva to kiva throughout the evening. Each group of dancers begins in its own home kiva and then visits other kivas throughout the night—returning to its own kiva for one last set.

In the lunar month of *Powamuya* (February), a major ceremony emphasizing the concept of germination takes place before fields are cleared and readied for planting. The Powamuy Ceremony, also known as the Bean Dance, is a sixteen-day ceremony that features the forced growth of bean sprouts in the warm atmosphere of the kiva. These sprouts foretell the coming growth of the crops. On the fifteenth day of the ceremony, the bean sprouts are taken from the kiva by the kachinas and distributed to the villagers—who then make them into a bean sprout soup.

Also associated with the Powamuy Ceremony is the coming of the *Sooso'yokt* or ogre kachinas. This group of horrible-looking kachinas goes from house to house, stopping to recite to each child all of his or her past misdeeds and failed obligations. They threaten to take the children from their homes and eat them. In exchange for the children's lives, parents and relatives offer the ogres large quantities of food along with promises of reform from the children. Initially, the ogres appear dissatisfied with these substitutions, saying, for example, that piiki bread will hurt their teeth or that they only crave the tender flesh of young children. Only after much food has been handed over and a promise or demonstration of

Hopi Ceremonial Wheel Calendar

KACHINA SEASON

- FEBRUARY — Powamuya "Bean Dance"
- MARCH — Kiva Dances
- APRIL — Plaza Dances
- MAY — Plaza Dances
- JUNE — Plaza Dances / 21st Summer Solstice
- JULY — Niman Home Dance

NON-KACHINA SEASON

- AUGUST — Snake or Flute Dance
- SEPTEMBER — Women's Society Dances
- OCTOBER — Women's Society Dances
- NOVEMBER — Wuwtsim / Tribal Initiation
- DECEMBER — 21st Winter Solstice / Soyalangw
- JANUARY — Kiva Dances

This Hopi ceremonial wheel calendar representing the alternating kachina and non-kachina seasons is derived from Barton Wright's *Hopi Kachinas: The Complete Guide* published by Northland Press in 1977.

5

Sooso'yokt Katsinam (ogre kachinas)
There are several ogre kachinas
that appear in association with the
Bean Dance in the lunar month of
Powamuya including:

ABOVE: *Nata'aska*, black ogre (E843)

INSET TOP LEFT: *Sooso'yoktuy Taaha'am*
(E682)

INSET LOWER LEFT: *So'yokwuuti*, a female
ogre kachina (E695).

good behavior has been extracted from the terrified child are the ogres persuaded to leave.

At the end of the day, the Hopi men make bets with the ogres, betting them, for example, that they cannot dance. It almost always turns out that the ogres lose the wagers and thus forfeit all of the food they have gathered up that day. This is one of the lighter moments of the day, and it brings the ceremony to a close.

In March, there is a second series of night kiva dances that often features the use of puppets as an added element. When the lunar month of *Ösömuya* (roughly March) ends and the weather again warms, the kachina dances move into the village plazas where they are held through the spring and early summer. In early spring, the dances can feature the appearance of a class of kachinas called *Wawarkatsinam*, or runner kachinas, who challenge the men to short foot races. Depending on the type of kachina, the consequences for losing can vary— but the result is usually unpleasant. For example, *Hömsona* will cut the loser's hair while *Wik'tsina* (or greasy kachina) will smear his face with the greasy black soot of a stove pipe. No matter who wins or loses, however, the runner kachina always gives his opponent a food gift in the end. The racing continues until the presents of food brought by the runners are used up. Then, a Hopi man serving as a spokesman for the villagers sprinkles the runner kachinas with corn meal and sends them off with a message for rain.

The dances themselves have a festive air. Preparations begin long in advance since great quantities of food must be readied. The day of the ceremony begins early. First, long lines of kachinas perform the ritual dances, singing and moving in unison though dance steps are often complex. After returning from

breaks, the kachinas may give away large quantities of food. Noontime usually brings an invitation to share a meal that includes a stew called *nöqkwivi* consisting of corn hominy and mutton.

The plaza dances very often feature visits by the *Tsutskut* (or Hopi clowns). These clowns arrive in the early afternoon on the first day of a two-day plaza dance. They go through a series of standard actions and activities that reflect the lifecycle of a human being. The clowns are different at each mesa. Their faces are painted in a style distinctive to that mesa—and they do not wear masks. Thus, they are not considered kachinas. (Likewise, a kachina may seem funny in action or appearance, but if it has a mask, it is considered a kachina and not a clown by the Hopi.) The clowns provide comic relief during the day when the kachinas have gone to the *k'atsinki* or kachina house (usually a hidden brush- or wall-lined area) to rest. Although the clowns are funny, they have a serious purpose, for they spoof those who have violated the conventions of Hopi society— and thus make fun of un-Hopi or *"qahopi"* behavior.

On the afternoon of the final day of the two-day plaza dance, the clowns are warned by a group of kachinas called *kipok* or raider kachinas to shape up. The warnings of these *kipokkatsinam* are ignored, however, and in the end the raiders must punish (and thus symbolically purify) the clowns for their

ABOVE: *Tasavu*, or Navajo clown kachina (E2498). This kachina often functions as a *pusukintaqa*—or drummer—for other kachinas.

7

reckless, un-Hopilike behavior. Even though the clowns provide much amusement, their ultimate fate at the hands of the *kipokkatsinam* always provides an object lesson about the consequences of being "*qahopi*."

Following the summer solstice, the Niman (or Going-Home) Ceremony begins. This sixteen-day rite, which except for the final day takes place in the secrecy of the kiva, ends the kachina season. On the final day of the ceremony, *Nimantikive* or Niman dance day, the kachinas appear in public for the last time during the year. On this occasion, the first green corn crops are presented to the people of the village by the kachinas—who dance one last time for rain to spur on the final growth of the remaining crops. Having helped the Hopi through midsummer, the kachinas return to their own realm to begin the cycle anew.

HOPI KACHINA DOLLS

Kachina dolls or *tihu* (*tithu* in the plural) are carved representations of kachina spirits. Made of cottonwood roots, they are traditionally fashioned as gifts from the kachinas to uninitiated girls. Originally, the gifts served a purpose similar to the *paaho* (prayer stick) out of which they may have evolved. When a little girl received one, it was, in effect, a prayer-wish that she would grow, be healthy and fertile, and in turn have healthy children of her own.

Infant girls receive their first doll in the form of a *putsqatihu*, a flat kachina doll representing *Hahay'iwuuti*, the "mother of the kachinas," who is said to embody all of the qualities of a good mother. In some villages, infant boys may also receive this *putsqatihu*. These dolls are usually presented at the Powamuy Ceremony (the Bean Dance) and at the Niman (or Going-Home Ceremony), again, as a fertility prayer-wish.

When young girls receive kachina dolls, they either play with them, or the dolls are hung on the wall to serve as a reminder of the kachinas. Some flat dolls are tied to miniature cradle boards and played with as a doll and cradle set.

The oldest known kachina dolls date to the early eighteenth century though it is likely that the form is even more ancient in Hopi culture. These earliest *tithu* are flat, as are the infant dolls of today, with a simple break separating the head from the body. The earliest examples of painted kachina dolls reveal that the head was painted with the characteristic markings of the particular kachina. The body was painted simply, usually with a white base and three red stripes.

Over the past century, kachina dolls have evolved in form and function. This evolution began with a greater elaboration of the head. This was followed by

ABOVE: *Mongwa,* or great horned owl kachina (E659). This figure is the leader of the raider kachinas.

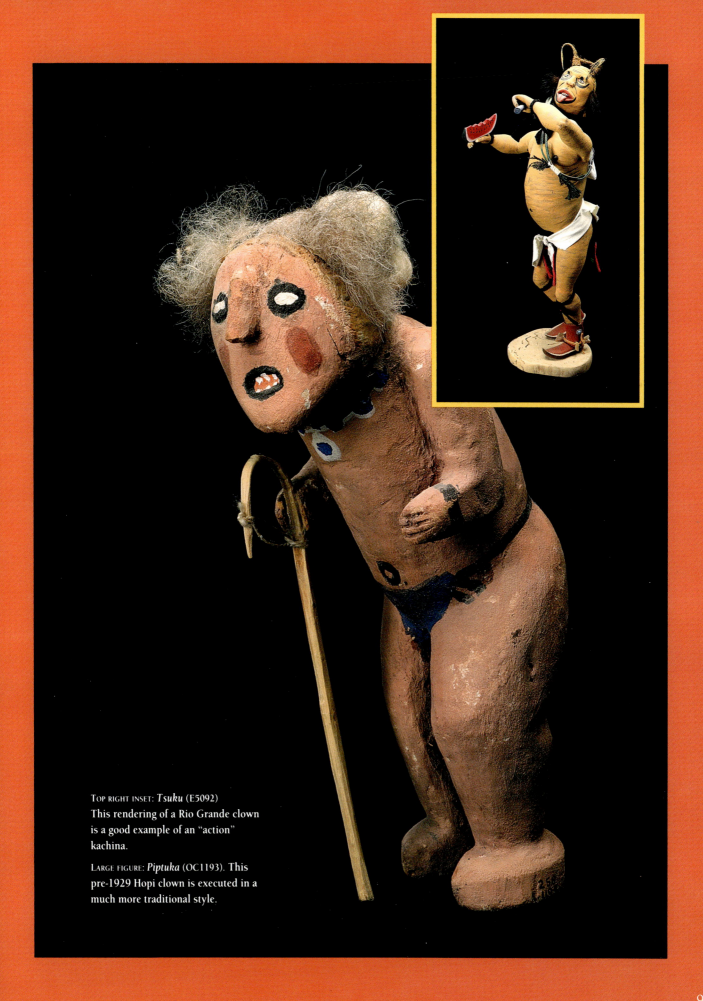

TOP RIGHT INSET: *Tsuku* (E5092)
This rendering of a Rio Grande clown
is a good example of an "action"
kachina.

LARGE FIGURE: *Piptuka* (OC1193). This
pre-1929 Hopi clown is executed in a
much more traditional style.

a sculptural definition of the arms and legs. Older dolls of the sculptural type usually have arms and legs that conform to the cylindrical shape of the cottonwood root. Arms were attached to the body—running down the sides of the doll, bending at the elbows, and meeting in front. The Hopi call dolls done in this style *ponotutuyqa*—"one with a stomach ache." Early legs were made with a simple vertical split up the middle of the doll. Body painting on very early sculptural pieces remained the same as on the flat dolls (a white base and red stripes). Later, pieces were carved and painted in a style that depicted the full costume of the kachina, with a flaring wooden skirt carved to represent the kilt and two short legs projecting below.

Early dolls had a base cover of white clay (kaolin) and were painted with mineral paints including oxides of iron, copper ores, and colored clays. Near the turn of the century, these paints gave way to a variety of commercially made paints introduced by traders. Tempera paint or poster paints soon became well established and remained the most popular paints until the more recent introduction of acrylic paints.

Non-Hopi people have been purchasing kachina dolls for over a century. This has been done despite the fact that there was initial Hopi resistance to selling kachina dolls. It was felt by many Hopi then, and indeed by some today, that it was "like selling your children." The commercial sale of *tithu* has been, how-

ever, a major factor in the evolution of the kachina doll. Near the end of World War II, carvers began creating dolls that revealed more of the kachina dancer's action. Modern "action" dolls are carved in poses characteristic of a particular kachina and often show great detail—including musculature and even fingernails. Because the pieces show motion, they are far more likely to have glued-on appendages than to be fashioned from one piece of wood though some carvers still pride themselves on working from a single piece of wood. Today, too, new materials are in use; for example, green yarn is often used to simulate the evergreen ruff just below the head of the kachina doll. Some recent kachina dolls even carry plastic evergreens or flowers. Feathers are more likely to be carved of wood now since the feathers of appropriate birds cannot be attached to dolls for sale to non-Indians.

The commercial development of kachina doll carving also has resulted in the breaking of some traditional taboos. Traditionally, kachina dolls were carved out of the view of children, as the *tithu* were to be gifts from the supernatural kachinas. This practice has been widely discarded, however, and dolls, frequently made to order, are carved openly in the home. Likewise, as gifts from the kachinas, dolls were never signed in traditional times. This prohibition was evidently broken by Jimmie Kewanwytewa, who signed many of his dolls with his initials, "J.K." in the 1950s. Today, dolls made for sale very often are

Hahay'iwuti (E66A). A *putsqatihu* or flat kachina doll that is often the first doll given to young girls.

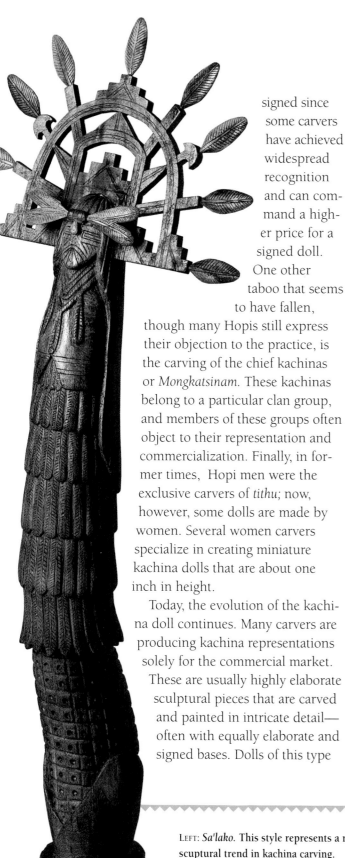

signed since some carvers have achieved widespread recognition and can command a higher price for a signed doll.

One other taboo that seems to have fallen, though many Hopis still express their objection to the practice, is the carving of the chief kachinas or *Mongkatsinam*. These kachinas belong to a particular clan group, and members of these groups often object to their representation and commercialization. Finally, in former times, Hopi men were the exclusive carvers of *tithu;* now, however, some dolls are made by women. Several women carvers specialize in creating miniature kachina dolls that are about one inch in height.

Today, the evolution of the kachina doll continues. Many carvers are producing kachina representations solely for the commercial market. These are usually highly elaborate sculptural pieces that are carved and painted in intricate detail—often with equally elaborate and signed bases. Dolls of this type have great commercial value—and are far removed from the *tithu* of old. Indeed, they might be more properly described as kachina sculptures since they now serve none of the functions of the original *tithu*. One of the more significant recent developments is unpainted kachina sculpture. With these pieces, the emphasis is on the sculptural quality of the figures and on the look of the wood grain. In some instances, these pieces are partially painted to highlight portions of the face or the clothing. This emphasis on sculpture is, in fact, leading some carvers completely away from the kachina effigy form. Some are now specializing in fashioning unpainted sculptural works that combine a variety of kachina faces with other kinds of symbolic forms such as corn, clouds, lightning, and fertility motifs.

In reaction to these developments, one Hopi carver began carving kachina dolls in the older, simpler *ponotutuyqa* "stomach ache" style using soft colors that give the dolls an antique look. This carver, who started making these dolls as a "protest" against the rococo nature of the modern doll, has initiated a new movement in kachina carving. His works have found a ready market among those who favor the earthy simplicity of the old *tihu*.

LEFT: *Sa'lako*. This style represents a new scuptural trend in kachina carving. Frequently, all or part of the figure is stained or is left unpainted. Photograph courtesy of Horizons West

ABOVE RIGHT: *Saviki* (E6194). This kachina exemplifies a gradual transition to greater detailing in the kachina figure.

Four excellent examples of an earlier, simpler style.

INSETS:

TOP LEFT: *Hilili* (E2280)

BOTTOM LEFT: *Ang'ak'china*, or long-haired kachina (E2277)

BOTTOM RIGHT: *Kokosori* (E2288)

LARGE FIGURE: *Palhikwmana* (E2284)

All of these developments by Hopi carvers have been affected by another recent trend—carving of Hopilike kachina dolls by non-Hopi carvers. Produced solely for commercial purposes by other Indian people, and to a lesser extent by non-Indians, these dolls usually only approximate the look of the Hopi kachina, for their carvers are not culturally familiar with the details of how a Hopi kachina should look. Many are grotesque and almost mocking imitations of Hopi kachina dolls. Because they are usually cheaper than authentic Hopi kachinas, they are sold widely.

In another early break with tradition, some carvers fashioned effigies of non-kachina forms—such as the buffalo dancer, kokopelli, and snake and flute society members. Because these forms do not represent kachinas and would not be presented to little girls in Hopi ceremonies, they are not properly called *tithu* or kachina dolls.

Navankatsina. This doll typifies the modern or "action" doll.

I was born in the Hopi village of Bacavi on Third Mesa. In World War II, I served in the 114th Construction Battalion in France and Germany. Today, I am a farmer, a kachina carver, and (during the Hopi dances) a Father of the Kachinas, taking care of the kachinas between dances.

I have been carving a long time. My first interest was in the old kachinas whose names I knew. These were the ones I began to carve. No one taught me how; I just learned by doing.

My dolls are done in the traditional ways: carving in one piece and putting feathers on them. I always carve my dolls in the standing position, beginning at the feet and working up. Since some collectors like my unique style, I don't want to make any drastic changes in the way I carve or to experiment with new models. I view most of my carvings as traditional art—that's my favorite. I am proud that some collectors like my style; it makes me feel wonderful about my carvings.

I don't carve regularly because I farm a piece of land in Tuba City. Farming is hard work, and it takes a lot of time. Mostly, I carve when I need money to buy things. Since my carvings are collector's items, I have never had to go far to market them. Currently, I sell them only at the Museum of Northern Arizona, and I try to keep the museum stocked with my items.

I have a place in my house where I can work alone, with my radio on. I'll work until I get tired, then I'll rest and carve more. Sometimes, I'll do as many as six carvings at a time. My dolls range from miniature up to nine inches, but most are between seven and nine inches tall.

Getting wood for the dolls is a big job. Some carvers buy wood, but I get my own. About four years ago, I was returning from my daughter's wedding in North Dakota and stopped under a bridge in Craig, Colorado, for lunch. The creek there was full of driftwood—cottonwood roots, which is what kachina dolls are carved out of. I didn't have a chainsaw with me, so I chopped the wood with my ax. I brought home as much as I could load, and I'm still using that wood.

I use several knives for carving. I like the Old Timer knives, in particular. I usually have one favorite knife that I've learned to hide when my grandsons come over. Of all of my knives, somehow, they'd pick my favorite to put in their pocket. Then, they'd take it out in the yard and lose it, so I'd never see it again.

I have three sons who are all good kachina carvers: Wilburt Talashoma, Jr., who lives in Santa Fe, New Mexico; Tott Talashoma, who lives in Polacca, Arizona; and Lowell Talashoma, a well-known carver who lives at Second Mesa in Arizona. My sons learned how to carve on their own; I didn't teach them. It would be too hard to teach someone else to carve—you just have to get used to it. I was the first person to become a kachina carver in my family, and I guess I started a new tradition.

Wilburt Talashoma.
Photograph by Cindy Young

was born May 1, 1942, in the Hopi village of Moenkopi. For about twenty years, I worked as a bricklayer. But when jobs became scarce, I had to find another way to support myself and my family—that is how I fell into kachina carving.

Looking back, I can see I was born with an artistic ability. As early as grade school, I knew I had some kind of gift. During the sixth grade, all I did was sketch kachinas. Later, I began doing watercolor paintings of kachina dolls, painting from memory the kachinas I had seen during the dances held when I was a child. To perfect my paintings and give them detail, I studied human anatomy in medical books and Michelangelo's drawings of the human body.

In 1967, I was drafted into the army and went to Vietnam. I continued to do artwork there—sketching for people. Mostly, I drew portraits of my friends or of their wives or girlfriends. I began my career as a journeyman bricklayer when I returned from Vietnam. During my lunch break, I would pick up a brick and sketch powdery designs on it with the white pencil I used to mark bricks for cutting.

Once, between bricklaying jobs, I went to help my uncle on his ranch. My uncle was Wilson Kaye, a carver well known for his mudheads. He encouraged me to try carving. Although it wasn't something I was very interested in, I needed the money so I tried it. The Museum of Northern Arizona bought both of my first carvings for $100 each, which was a lot of money to me. The buyer told me my carvings were pretty good for a first-timer and said she thought I might have possibilities as a carver. That's when the fever started.

I began to explore the possibility of becoming a carver. Since I didn't know much about carving, I knew it wouldn't be easy. First, I studied kachina dolls

everywhere. Then, I began visiting other carvers. I would watch them carve and try to trick them into telling me their techniques. But I didn't copy them. Instead, I pushed myself to develop my own style.

What makes my carvings unique are the emotions I work into the doll. I make sure the dolls are not just standing there. Nearly everyone who sees my kachina dolls tells me they immediately sense the strong emotion coming from the doll. One woman at the Indian Market in Santa Fe actually jumped when she turned around and saw one of my ogre dolls.

Carving gives me great satisfaction even though it is sometimes painstaking. When I see the finished product, I am always motivated to do more. Often, as soon as I deliver a kachina doll to the buyer, my hands are itching to begin again. New ideas for carvings are constantly brewing in my head. In the future, I would like to do larger carvings with more story to them, but they will take more time and larger pieces of wood.

Carving is just one part of my life. I am also a farmer and am very involved in the Hopi ceremonials. I usually get up at 3:00 A.M. to carve before the working day begins. It's comfortable to be carving then because I can really concentrate. Sometimes, I think I would like to do only carving, but my family farmed and raised livestock—and it is in me.

To me, carving is a beautiful art, a gift I can give to people. I feel lucky this gift was revealed to me and that I can bring a little bit of beauty into this world.

Loren Phillips holding recent carving of Eagle Kachina. Photograph by Chester Lewis

Wilburt Talashoma's kachinas illustrate a simpler, classic style that reflects traditional kachina carvings. It remains popular with both Hopi carvers and collectors.

ABOVE, RIGHT: *Cumulus Cloud Kachina.*

INSET: Three small carvings by Wilburt Talashoma including a *koshare, ho'ote, and qööqöqlö.* Photographs by Cindy Young

Loren Phillips' figures, also popular with collectors, exemplify a trend toward greater detail and emotion.

LEFT: A ram kachina. Photograph by Chester Lewis

INSET: An eagle kachina. Photograph by Jerry Sinkovec

Note: *Bill Beaver is owner of Sacred Mountain Trading Post on U.S. Highway 89 twenty-five miles north of Flagstaff. He offers the following suggestions from what he has learned during fifty years of collecting kachina figures and helping others build kachina collections.*

How do you begin to collect Hopi kachina figures?* Although the process may seem obvious—just purchase the doll and add it to your collection—some questions immediately arise. How many kachina figures should a person have in a collection? What are some specific "themes" that might be pursued? How can you learn about kachinas? And what price should you pay?

The question "How many kachinas make up a complete collection?" can only be answered by another: "What is complete?" In truth, there is probably no good answer to this question. The Hopi religion has so many kachinas that I know of no one anywhere who owns figures of all of them. Some museums in the United States and in other countries certainly hold impressive collections, but they are still not complete in the sense of having examples of every type. If a number must be settled upon, a collection of three hundred to four hundred kachinas would be very complete, though that number probably could be doubled.

This question of completeness can be illustrated by specific situations. Many of the same kachinas, such as the Cow and Hummingbird, are made in different colors. Does a collector need to own one of each color—or is that unnecessary duplication? In a similar vein, some kachinas are carved in both male and female forms. Would you need to double the size of a collection for the sake of completeness? These questions are most troublesome for beginning collectors.

To avoid these problems, collectors often specialize. One person I know collects only female kachinas, while another purchases only animal kachinas. Others seek only those made by a particular carver. What is most important is that the collection contain kachina dolls that mean something to the collector.

A collector will soon become aware of variations among kachina figures. These differences may be small or quite distinct; they may be rooted in village tradition or individual choice. Many times a carver will respond to a request for a kachina doll by saying, "I don't know that kachina because that's from another village." Often, a kachina appears the same in a number of villages, but one village will produce it in

---

LOWER LEFT: *Angwusnasomtaqa* (E686). A central figure in the Powamuy or Bean Dance Ceremony.

UPPER RIGHT: *Navakchin'mana*, or snow maiden (E3809).

* The terms "doll" and "figure" are used here interchangeably. The word "doll" has come into the language through long, common usage. However, it should be noted that kachina figures are in no sense statues or idols.

a unique form. I encourage collectors to acquire the unique ones, as well as one example of the more representative type. On the other hand, names for the same kachina vary among villages. In this case, the dialectic differences would not warrant the purchase of each separately named kachina.

One variation I point out to collectors and dealers involves the popular mudheads. At the Hopi dances, several different types of mudheads appear at different rituals, and they have specific functions. Thus, a comprehensive collection should include at least some of these different mudheads. To complicate this, however, mudheads appear in other kachinas' costumes. To acquire all of these would mean a great increase in the number of kachina dolls in a collection. One or two of these variations would be satisfactory—in my personal collections, for instance, I have a long hair and a badger mudhead.

Most collections contain some dolls that are not truly kachinas. One of the most appealing to collec-

tors is the Snake Dancer. Less common are the Antelope Priest depiction and, occasionally, a figure of the Flute Priest. Various clowns, such as the *Koyalla* (or *Koshare*), are depicted as well. These black-and-white striped clowns are particular favorites for today's collectors.

As collections grow, a practical consideration arises—lack of

space to display the figures. Years ago, many collectors followed the Hopi practice of hanging kachina dolls from the roof rafters or on the wall. Strings around the necks of older dolls are there for this purpose. Later, carvers put the kachina figures on stands or bases so they could be placed on shelves.

Although this change may seem fairly insignificant, at one time the Museum of Northern Arizona would not judge a kachina doll for prizes if it appeared on a stand. The judges considered such figures untraditional and commercial. Some collectors also resisted buying a kachina on a stand because they wanted only those dolls that had been handed out to girls during the dances. Now, however, kachina dolls rarely appear without a stand because consumers will not buy them.

One solution to the problem of space is to collect flat slab kachinas. Like full kachina figures, the flat slab types are carved and painted, but the bodies are greatly abbreviated. Most importantly, they retain the single most important identifying feature of any kachina, the face. For the collector there are advantages: because flat slab figures are smaller, a great number of them can be displayed on a wall. And a good collection of them can be accumulated at much less cost.

LOWER LEFT: *Owangaroro*, angry or stone eater kachina.

UPPER RIGHT: *Kokopelli*, or humpback flute player (E897B).

Mudhead kachinas. Since *Kooyemsim* (or mudheads) are masked, they are properly considered kachinas rather than clowns. Many collections focus on these popular figures.

TOP RIGHT INSET: *Kooyemsit*—(plural form), or mudheads (E3864 and E3728).

BOTTOM RIGHT INSET: *Kooyemsi*—(singular form), or mudhead (E8554).

LEFT: *Kuwan Powamu Koyemsi* (OC1177).

ABOVE RIGHT: *Navankatsina* (E2293). A simpler style of a velvet-shirt kachina than that shown on page 13.

LEFT: *Wuyaqtaywa* (E9479). An example of the new "old-style" kachinas gaining in popularity.

The age of a kachina figure can be another attribute to guide a collector. When I started collecting, I knew carvers who had been born in the late 1800s.

Their work represented a style that was passing, and I sought out these figures partly because I knew they were becoming scarce. Equally important was the fact that these carvers had actually seen many of the kachinas, had participated in the dances, and knew their stories.

Older carvings, even though they are unsigned and are not placed on stands, have definite appeal. One feature of the older dolls is that real bird feathers were used. In the late 1960s and early 1970s, however, controversy arose over the use of feathers from protected birds such as eagles. Stores were afraid to handle kachina figures that might have used illegal feathers; consequently, sales dropped sharply. Carvers responded by switching to feathers from chicken, turkeys, and pheasants. Others now carve feathers of wood, with the advantage that carved feathers do not deteriorate.

Styles of kachina carvings have changed through the years. Kachina "sculptures" have come into vogue, and painting styles have changed as well. Many modern carvers now stain part of the kachina and leave the rest natural. Tools have changed, too, with electrical tools and woodburning devices being used more and more. In addition to changes in style, there have been changes in the actual figures carved. Younger carvers have not seen some of the older kachinas and thus do not make them.

Older style kachinas are really folk art, and most are now gone except those made by a few elderly carvers. Different values influence collectors these days. A major change occurred in the 1950s and 1960s, when what I call the "name game" gained prominence. That is, the value of a kachina doll began to rest with who had carved it, rather than whether it had been given out at a dance. Part of this came about with the addition of stands, where the carver could put a name and address and thus have a form of advertising. Partly this change was a function of the boom in growth in the Southwest, which has had both good and bad results. Knowledge and appreciation of Native American culture and crafts has grown dramatically in recent years. Since prices for crafts have increased correspondingly, there has been an unfortunate increase in the number of fraudulent reproductions as well. The fairly rapid shift from traditional to commercial in this artform has caused bewilderment, resentfulness, and competition. Some Hopi carvers resent the high prices consumers pay for dolls that they do not consider better than their own. Because the money to be made in kachina figures is determined almost entirely in the outside market, carvers are increasingly subject to the caprice of trends set by galleries and the southwestern craft market.

OPPOSITE: Left figure is *Si'ohemiskatsina* (E7312). Right figure is *Hemiskatsina* (E2396). These Niman kachinas are most commonly seen at the Niman or Going Home Dance.

ABOVE: *Hakto* (E3873). Because early dolls like this one were designed to hang on the wall or be used as a doll, they were not placed on stands.

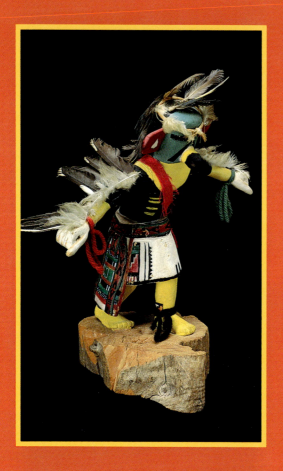

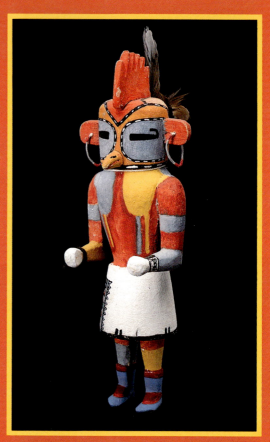

BUYING KACHINAS

Where is the best place to buy kachina dolls? It is fairly easy to visit any of the villages at Hopi if one observes the requirements of each village and is always respectful of people's privacy. Signs in the windows of homes in most villages indicate if kachina dolls are sold. You also may ask a Hopi resident you see outside. Polite and helpful people, they will tell you where crafts can be purchased. Kachina carvers also live in towns near the Hopi Reservation.

Kachina figures can be purchased at craft fairs and Indian markets held at various times of the year in Arizona and New Mexico. The three largest and best-known markets are the Museum of Northern Arizona's Hopi Show held each year during the Fourth of July weekend, the All-Indian Market held in August in Santa Fe, and December's Indian Market at the Pueblo Grande Museum in Phoenix. At these markets and fairs, you will have many opportunities to ask about specific kachinas at booths operated by Hopi families. You also can learn of other upcoming shows.

Another source of kachina dolls are the many privately owned shops and trading posts located along the highways and in larger cities and resort towns in the Southwest. Some private concessionaire shops also may be found within national parks in the region.

If you are inclined to collect older kachinas, auctions are good sources. They are held at various times in different parts of the country from San Francisco to New York. Many older kachinas come onto the market by way of estate sales, from collections being liquidated, and from gallery closeouts. While these are the most obvious sources, I have heard of some very nice kachinas found at garage sales! The moral is that great kachinas and great buys are where you find them.

Anyone seriously contemplating a kachina collection should visit as many of these sources as possible. Do your homework. Look at various kachinas, see what you like, compare prices, and ask questions. Although you may receive some contradictory information along the way, that is part of the education of a collector. Persistent investigation will pay off. You will get a sense of the marketplace, the style (or styles) you may wish to purchase, and the wide variation in prices.

This knowledge, along with advice from experts, will help you be assured that the kachina figure is authentic. Knowing the dealer and the carver are ways to avoid being taken in by a fake. Two other characteristics you might look for are the wood used and the painting. The traditional material from which kachina dolls are carved is cottonwood root. And the face painting and body painting should correspond. If a certain kachina always wears blue shoes, for example, you would not expect to see it rendered with red shoes. Also be aware that if you see a number of kachina dolls lined up on a shelf, all about the

---

OPPOSITE: **Bird kachinas remain popular with both carvers and collectors. Examples include:**
ABOVE LEFT: *Kwa,* **or eagle kachina (E8553).**
ABOVE RIGHT: *Kowaako,* **or rooster kachina (OC1184).**
LOWER LEFT: *Pawiki,* **or duck kachina (E639).**
LOWER RIGHT: *Kisa,* **or prairie falcon kachina (E3169).**

ABOVE: *Tsa'kwaynam* **(crescent eyes E955) (middle figure E3758) (figure on left E3827). This kachina character, borrowed from Zuni, is a very popular kachina believed to predate the coming of the Spanish.**

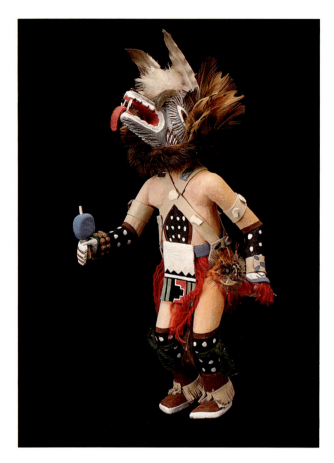

any market, a figure listed at a thousand dollars would be an expensive kachina. A good doll, eight to fifteen inches high, on average would be priced between $150 and $500.

Remember, though, that a "good deal" is in the eye of the buyer. About the only "rule" I can make is that if the kachina is one you want, and the price is right for you, it is a good buy.

A KACHINA COLLECTOR'S BIBLIOGRAPHY

Any collector will want to read as much as possible about kachinas. Fortunately, a number of good books that follow closely the evolution of Hopi culture, both archaeologically and ethnologically, are available. Some are organized according to the ceremonial calendar of the Hopi, others by the function of the kachina.

Books have played an especially important role in the making, buying, selling, and collecting of kachina figures. Often, orders are given carvers by individuals who specify a kachina they have seen in a book. For this reason, everyone—dealers, store owners, collectors, and even the carvers—buy the books. But at times, things get out of control, and the carvers' creativity is affected. A kachina figure may not sell because it is not illustrated in the standard books— or if the figure does not look exactly like the one shown in the book. And a mistake in the illustration of a kachina can be perpetuated and standardized if it is copied.

No one book contains *all* the kachinas. That would be an overwhelming task because there are an incredible number of kachinas in the religious world of the Hopi.

The earliest publication on kachinas is the Smithsonian Institution's *Twenty-first Annual Report of 1903.*

same size, in the same pose, and around the same low price, these could be mass-produced, non-Hopi kachinas.

Prices for kachinas are based on the amount of carving as well as the size of the actual figure. Price will depend also upon who did the carving since kachina carvers themselves have become a commodity. Reputation and publicity are often the determiners of market value. Kachinas that have won ribbons in shows are also higher priced. And prices depend, too, on where you buy the doll. Even with all these provisos, a range of prices can be stated. In nearly

ABOVE: *Kweo*, or wolf kachina (E5426). One of the most dramatic kachina figures—and therefore popular with collectors.

OPPOSITE, INSET: *Kipokkatsinam*, or raider kachinas. *Tsorporyaqahöntaqa* (blue face) (E894B) and *Eewero* (E895). These kachinas punish the *tsuskut*, or clowns, for their un-Hopilike behavior.

LARGE FIGURE: *Wuyak'ku* (E7546a). This broad-faced kachina appears at the Bean Dance.

Archaeologist Jesse Walter Fewkes wrote it in the late 1890s. The paintings it includes were done by several Hopi from First Mesa. In the publication, the kachinas are arranged largely as they appeared in ceremonies performed at First Mesa. An exceptionally well-done book, it is highly recommended to collectors if a copy can be found through a used book store or buyer. It was reprinted in 1962 by the Rio Grande Press under the title *Hopi Katcinas: Drawn by Native Artists*.

Second is Harold S. Colton's *Hopi Kachina Dolls: with a Key to their Identification,* originally published by the University of New Mexico Press in 1949 and revised in 1959. Although this book does not contain color renditions of the kachinas, it is the major reference for collecting kachina figures. Colton's book is far more comprehensive than Fewkes' because Colton covers all the villages and refers to earlier publications.

Another well-known source is *Hopi Kachinas: The Complete Guide to Collecting Kachina Dolls* by Barton Wright (Northland Press, 1977). In this book, Wright groups the kachinas by function, roughly in the same classification the Hopi would use. This book contains good color illustrations of actual kachina figures. Wright includes both Hopi kachina names and English equivalents and cross-references them.

In 1973 Northland Press with the Heard Museum in Phoenix published Kachinas: *A Hopi Artist's Documentary*. This book contains original paintings by Cliff Bahnimptewa with text by Barton Wright. It is now used extensively as a source for information

ABOVE: *Tasapkatsinam*, or Navajo kachinas (left to right—E957, E2276, E638). Many kachinas bear the names of other Indian tribes such as Navajo, Comanche, Havasupai, and Apache. These names are not kachinas belonging to these tribes. Instead, they are Hopi kachinas that embody the spirits of these tribes.

and for ordering kachina figures. Dealers and collectors also compare potential purchases against the pictures in the book.

This book reflects a subtle change that has taken place in the world of kachina collection—the almost exclusive use of Hopi names for the kachinas. This has resulted in a sort of esoteric club among buyers and collectors that could intimidate people who want to read and learn more about kachina figures and the kachina religion.

In 1975 the Heard Museum published *Kachinas: The Barry Goldwater Collection at the Heard Museum.* Text is by Barton Wright. Curiously, although this book is not used as much by dealers and collectors as the previous one is, it seems to me to be a very good book for collectors. It shows actual figures collected over a long time period, at least from 1916 to the 1950s, and illustrates well the changes in carvings and painting styles that have transpired over the years. When I viewed the actual Goldwater collection, I was impressed by its reflection of the "pre-tourist" period. The collection would be nearly impossible to replace today.

One of the newest books on kachina dolls is by Arizona State Museum photographer Helga Teiwes, entitled *Kachina Dolls: The Art of Hopi Carvers.* This book was published by the University of Arizona Press in 1991 and includes text and photographs by Teiwes and historic photos by Forman Hanna.

Two other publications deserve mention for their tremendous photographs: *The Year of the Hopi; Paintings and Photographs by Joseph Mora, 1904-06* and *The Hopi Photographs: Kate Cory: 1905-1912.* Both include photographs of places at Hopi that no longer exist and kachina dancers that can never be seen again.

Aholi, or kachina chief's lieutenant (E688). This figures appears at Bean Dance in the company of *Eototo.*

30

There are probably as many reasons for collecting kachina dolls as there are collections—and as many ways. What I have presented are not "rules," but rather considerations to help sort out some of the possibilities. A well-defined objective or a specialization of some kind can help guide you. But individual collectors should not be swayed by trends or feel bound by the agendas that might influence institutions. The best advice I can offer is to enjoy putting your collection together—and collect what **you** like.

OPPOSITE: *Na'nga sohu,* or chasing star (E2647).

ABOVE: *Susopa,* or cricket kachina (E2499).

About The Authors

Robert G. Breunig, former Curator of Anthropology at the Museum of Northern Arizona, is now director of the Desert Botanical Garden in Phoenix, Arizona. Michael Lomatuway'ma was a native of Hotevilla, Arizona, a linguist and cultural consultant on the Hopi, and a member of the Powamuy Society.

Suggested Reading

Colton, Harold S. *Hopi Kachina Dolls: with a Key to Their Identification.* Albuquerque, New Mexico: University of New Mexico Press, 1959.

Dockstader, Frederick J. *The Kachina and The White Man.* Bloomfield Hills, Michigan: Cranbrook Institute of Science, Bulletin 35, 1954.

Earle, Edwin and Edward A. Kennard. *Hopi Kachinas.* New York: J. J. Augustis, 1938.

Erickson, Jon T. *Kachinas, An Evolving Hopi Art Form?* Phoenix, Arizona: The Heard Museum, 1977.

Fewkes, J. Walter. *Hopi Katcinas.* Washington, D.C.: Bureau of American Ethnology, 21st Annual Report. 1903.

Kabotie, Fred and Bill Belknap. *Fred Kabotie: Hopi Indian Artist.* Flagstaff, Arizona: Museum of Northern Arizona, 1977.

Malotki, Ekkehart. *Hopi Tales: A Bilingual Collection of Hopi Indian Stories.* Flagstaff, Arizona: Museum of Northern Arizona, 1978.

Thompson, Laura and Alice Joseph. *The Hopi Way.* Chicago, Illinois: University of Chicago Press, 1944.

Titiev, Mischa. *Old Oraibi.* Cambridge, Massachusetts: Peabody Museum of American Archaeology and Ethnology, Harvard University Papers, 1944.

Washburn, Dorothy K. "Hopi Kachinas: Spirit of Life," *American Indian Art*, Vol. 5, No. 3 (Summer 1980), pp. 48–53.

Wright, Barton A. *Hopi Kachinas, The Complete Guide to Collecting Kachina Dolls.* Flagstaff, Arizona: Northland Press, 1977.

Wright, Barton A. *Kachinas, A Hopi Artist's Documentary.* Flagstaff, Arizona: Northland Press, 1973.

Wright, Barton A. and Evelyn Roat. *This is a Hopi Kachina.* Flagstaff, Arizona: Museum of Northern Arizona, 1965.

Plateau Managing Editor: Diana Clark Lubick
Graphic Design: Julie Sullivan
Editorial Assistant: Donna A. Boyd
Electronic Imaging: Northland Printing
Color Separations: American Color
Printing: Land O'Sun

Note: All photographs not otherwise credited are by Gene Balzer. The E number designations in the captions indicate the catalog number in the Museum of Northern Arizona Collections.

COVER PHOTOGRAPH: *Avatshoya* (E2483).
Photograph by Gene Balzer